At
Cross
With
Jesus

10 Sermons And Monologues

Carl B. Rife and
Harold D. Shaffer

CSS Publishing Company, Inc., Lima, Ohio

AT THE CROSS WITH JESUS

For more information about CSS Publishing Company resources, visit our website at www.csspub.com.

ISBN 0-7880-1886-8
PRINTED IN U.S.A.

Table Of Contents

The Symbols Of The Cross
A Sermon Series For Lent
by **Carl B. Rife**

Foreword   9

Notes   10

The Palms   11
symbol of the fickleness of the crowd

The Money Bag   14
symbol of greed and attempt to manipulate Jesus

The Towel   20
symbol of servanthood

The Crown Of Thorns   24
symbol of mockery

The Nails   27
symbol of suffering

Five Who Knew Jesus
Monologues For Lent
by **Harold D. Shaffer**

Introduction	35
Prologue	36
John	38
Mary (The Mother Of Jesus)	42
Peter	46
Judas	51
Mary Magdalene	55

The
Symbols
Of The Cross

Dedicated to Joan Gartrell, a member of Hughes United Methodist Church, Wheaton, Maryland, and a member of its worship committee, who was responsible for obtaining the symbols, working out the dramatic scenarios, and recruiting the persons to carry out the action part of this sermon series. She helped to make the sermon series come alive. Her help in this sermon series and in other areas in the life and work of the church was invaluable to me.

Foreword

The sermon series *The Symbols Of The Cross* came into being through my collaboration with the worship committee at Hughes United Methodist Church in Wheaton, Maryland. It was built on a similar series I had presented a few years earlier at Milford Mill Church in Baltimore, Maryland. The worship committee at Hughes Church helped me to work out the dramatic aspects of this series. The series attempts to relate the traditional Lenten symbols — palm leaves, money bag, towel and basin, crown of thorns, and nails — to the cross. Part of the message involves acting out the message with appropriate actions relating to these symbols. The last sermon leads up to the dramatic climax of the nails being pounded into the cross.

The cross itself is not a symbol of our faith. It is the reality at the heart of our faith. The cross is the place of Jesus' death. The cross is the place of our redemption. The cross mirrors the sin of humanity. The cross opens up God's love to the world. The cross is the place of a most unmitigated evil. The cross is the place of a most unalloyed good. The symbols of the cross point us to this reality.

Carl B. Rife

Notes

The cross is made from a dead Christmas tree (actually two trees). With the placing of each symbol on the cross, there is a bit of drama. The symbol is placed on the cross after the sermon.

Palm Leaves — A group of people enter the sanctuary from the rear waving palm leaves and shouting, "Hosanna!" They place two of the palm leaves on the cross and then put the rest at the foot of the cross.

Money Bag — The money bag is thrown by Judas into the sanctuary and then is picked up by a designated person in the congregation, who brings it forward and hangs it on the cross.

Towel — Two persons with a towel and basin and stool enter the chancel area. One washes and dries the other's feet and then drapes the towel in the traditional way on the cross. The basin is placed at the foot of the cross.

Crown of Thorns — The crown of thorns is brought forward on a purple pillow and is placed on the cross.

Nails — Nails are driven with great solemnity into pre-drilled holes in the cross. The hammer is placed at the foot of the cross.

The Palms

I would like to speak to you today about two parades that took place during the last week of Jesus' life. These two parades may not seem much like parades to you. They were rather impromptu and informal. And yet the basic ingredients of a parade are there in these occurrences in Jesus' life — a procession of people going down a street with people lined up to watch.

Let's look at the two parades:

The first parade took place on what we now call Palm Sunday. It consisted of Jesus riding a donkey accompanied by his twelve disciples and other followers. Not much of a parade really, but it drew a large crowd of people, many of whom were in Jerusalem to celebrate the Passover. Jesus had decided to face down his accusers who wanted to get him out of the picture. Jesus made a bold statement of who he was in God's scheme of things by acting out Zechariah's prophecy and choosing to enter Jerusalem riding on a lowly donkey. But the people misunderstood. They waved palm branches and cried out, "Hosanna! Blessed is he who comes in the name of the Lord. Blessed is the King of Israel. Hosanna!" You see, they thought that Jesus was a military or political leader who would overthrow Roman rule. Now that expectation had to be quite a stretch. Look at Jesus and his motley crew of disciples. How could anyone really expect them to overthrow the Roman army? How could anyone expect this group to mount a successful campaign against the irritating and irksome Romans?

The second parade took place on what we now call Good Friday. By then the palm branches had begun to dry and wilt and turn brown. It was not a parade of Jesus' planning and choice. It was a procession from the praetorium where Jesus had been tried by Pilate to a place called Golgotha where he was to be crucified. Those in the procession were Jesus, two criminals who were also going to

11

be crucified, a contingent of Roman soldiers, and eventually Simon of Cyrene, who as a bystander was conscripted into carrying Jesus' cross. Not much of a parade either, but it again drew a crowd to watch this procession. Many in this crowd were the same persons who had hailed Jesus at his first parade earlier in the week but now they called out for his crucifixion. His first parade was a sign of who they thought he was, and now they felt Jesus had misled and failed them. No one was waving palm branches this time. There were also some in the crowd who tried to be as inconspicuous as possible; these were Jesus' disciples, who looked on with confusion, fear, and despair. And there were such people as Mary his mother and Mary of Magdala, who were watching with aching and agonizing hearts the spectacle about which they could do nothing.

The interesting part about it is that these two parades turned out to be very different from what they seemed. The first parade seemed to be a conqueror's entrance; it turned into misunderstanding, confrontation, denial, betrayal, conviction, and death. The second parade seemed to be the forced march of a pathetic, misguided victim to the place of his death; it turned into redemption and resurrection.

The week started out with the green palms and ended with dried, brown, dead palms, and yet the palms that celebrate Jesus' procession never die. These two parades made a difference in the life of Jesus' followers and in the life of the world. The first parade led to the scattering of the disciples to save their own necks. The second parade led to the gathering of the disciples by the power of the Risen Christ to save the world. In these two parades the disciples came to a clear understanding of who Jesus was and who Jesus was not. They came to understand in what way Jesus would accomplish his purpose by the power of love and not by the power of force. They came to understand Jesus' words about being obedient unto death. They came to understand what was going on in both parades. And they came to experience the power of God's love through Jesus' death on the cross.

Because of these two strange parades and what they mean, countless persons through the years have turned around and started marching in the right direction. They have marched through life with a new purpose, a new strength, a new enthusiasm. Each parade in its way has contributed to an understanding of what God has done and is doing in this man Jesus who we call the Christ. And because of what transpired in the events surrounding these two parades, people have joined together to bring the message of God's truth and love to the world.

These two parades call us to come out of the crowds and become a part of Jesus' ongoing procession.

- A procession that involves pain and suffering and cross-bearing, and yet a procession that promises triumph over the negative forces of life.
- A procession that involves the need for courage, and yet a procession that promises strength for its participants.
- A procession that involves giving up those things we hold dear, and yet a procession that promises all we will ever need.
- A procession that may seem confusing and puzzling, and yet a procession that makes everything clear.
- A procession that looks like it is marching toward a dead end, and yet a procession that opens up everything.
- A procession that is marked by dead, dry, wilted palm branches, and yet a procession that allows us to wave fresh palms and shout anew, "Hosanna, blessed is he who comes in the name of the Lord!"

Come, join Jesus' parade. The electricity is in the air. It is a parade that can change your life and the life of the world. We do not march alone. We march with Jesus. We march with each other. Do not allow the parade to end at the cross.

The Money Bag

J udas — Judas Iscariot
It would have been better had I not been born.
Oh, Lord.
Judas — Judas Iscariot
I did the most dastardly thing.

Judas, what did you do?
You could have been strong like Andrew, James, John.
You could have been restored like Peter.

No, I was not like Peter.
I was like Pilate.
My hands contain blood.
That money — thirty pieces of silver — the price of a slave.
That's blood money.

What promise I had.
What a mistake I made.
Jesus had confidence in me.
He chose me to carry the purse.

Oh, yes, I took care of our bills from this bag, paid our
     taxes, and bought our food.
He trusts me — he trusts me with the money to be used
     only for the work of the kingdom.

Ah, yes, the kingdom.
Will I ever get it in my head that what he wants is a
     spiritual kingdom?

Spiritual kingdom.
What we need is a Messiah.
A Messiah with a sword, a club, a spear, an army.
A Messiah who will overthrow Rome, and get rid of
    Caesar.
I carry a dagger for this purpose.

Spiritual kingdom.
He preached we should love our enemies.
I wanted to kill them.
He preached we should love one another.
It's a dog-eat-dog world.

Spiritual kingdom.
Jesus was never overly concerned about material things.
There was a fateful day when over 5,000 followed him
    to the hill and sat down.
He preached to them.
He spoke gloriously and authoritatively of God.
When we paused to discern the time of day, it was
    time to eat.
But no one had anything.
I didn't have enough in my purse to feed 5,000.
Send them away.
We had to send them away.
Let them get their own.
Why should we give to them?

Spiritual kingdom.
That day in Bethany —
A woman with an alabaster jar of precious ointment
    came to Jesus and poured it on his head.
Precious ointment.
To what purpose such a waste?
I mean why pour costly ointment on anybody?
Even the son of God?
Why not sell the precious stuff and give the money to
    our purse?

Jesus said she did it for his burial!
He was always thinking of death.
He said, "He who seeks to save his life shall lose it,
    and whoever loses his life for my sake shall find it."

I wanted to live.
I liked life.
Or what I thought was life.

But Jesus insisted that he must go to Jerusalem
    and be delivered up by the chief priests and the scribes
    and the Pharisees and be crucified.

Three years — that's all he lasted.
What a Messiah.
Three years and he didn't even have an army.

Well, he did have a following.
A week before he was crucified, when he was going to Jerusalem,
    there was such a large crowd of people — women and children
    — following him you could scarcely hear anything but shouts —
    Hosanna! Hosanna! Blessed is he who comes in the name
    of the Lord. Hosanna!

They waved their palm branches.
They spread their garments before him.
They kept shouting, "Hosanna! Hosanna!"

I thought, at last he can establish his kingdom —
If he can only get them to overthrow the Roman guards.

But he walked away from all that.
He went into the temple.

Again I thought that it was going to happen.
He overthrew the tables of the money changers.
He began to wreck the place.

I didn't like that.
I was concerned about money.
Why waste it?
You get what you can, however you can.
You need money to feed an army.
You need money to buy protection and sometimes
    power.

But Jesus wasn't concerned about money.
He wanted a spiritual kingdom —
A kingdom in the hearts of people —
A kingdom that would control hate and lust and
    greed and selfishness.
Oh, how I wish I would have let that kingdom come
    to me.

During the last week
We disciples met in the Upper Room for a secret meeting.
And before we got down to anything really important,
    Jesus took a towel and basin and began to wash the
    disciples' feet.

If only I had given in at that time,
I could have saved myself from this hell.

Jesus could have saved me.
But Satan had his grip on me.

He said he was going to die.
Don't you see?
He said he would be delivered up by the scribes and
    Pharisees and be crucified.

What a way to go.
Crucifixion.

Oh, why did I ever have to be the one to do it?
It would have been better if I had never been born.

After the last supper,
I met some Parisees just as conniving as I.
They made a deal with me.
Thirty pieces of silver.

What a loot.
I jumped at the chance — thirty pieces of silver,
The price of a slave.

It's blood money.
I will betray him with a kiss.
I know where he is.
Praying — praying at a place in the Mount of Olives
    called Gethsemane.

Then I did it.
It was dark.
I kissed him.
Then I ran, ran as fast as I could.

Clanging swords.
Stomping clubs.
They beat him.
They delivered him to Pilate.

Oh, what a horrible mistake.
They crucified him.
He died on the cross, like a criminal.
He committed no sin.
It makes my blood tingle.
My blood — my blood is worthless.
My blood can spark no life.
His blood could save the world.

I must get rid of this money.
I don't want it.

Here, take it, you Pharisees.
Take this back — you deceivers — you helped to crucify him.

You think you can't take it.
Here, take it. (*Throw money bag into congregation.*)
I don't want it.

Still as of old
I by myself am priced.
For thirty pieces of silver
I sold myself
Not Christ.

The Towel

Look at the cross before you, the wilted palm branches symbolizing the fact that early in the last week of Jesus' life the crowds cheered him on with shouts of Hosanna and toward the end of the week their commitment wilted just like these palm branches. Then look at the money bag, the symbol of greed, yes, but also a symbol of the attempt of some people to manipulate Jesus to their understanding of who the Messiah really was.

In the portrayal of Judas there was a line that is easily overlooked. It went like this: "During the last week the disciples gathered in the Upper Room and *before we got down to anything really important*, Jesus took a towel and basin and began to wash the disciples' feet."

Before we got down to anything really important, Jesus took a towel and basin and began to wash the disciples' feet. That response by Judas was one perspective on the act of Jesus when he took a towel and basin and indeed washed the disciples' feet. From Judas' point of view, *the act was seen as an intrusion into the more important matters between Jesus and the disciples.*

Nothing could be further from the mark. The act was filled with the meaning of Jesus' life and ministry. The act communicated the essence of Jesus' life and mission to his disciples and later followers.

Far from being an unimportant intrusion into the matters at hand, it was a pregnant moment of maximum import. Here the ultimate met the intimate in this act of service and love. What could be more important than this kind of moment?

Let us look at what kind of moment this was.

It was a shocking moment. It was not what the disciples expected. Earlier the disciples had argued among themselves who would be greatest in the kingdom. When Jesus overheard them, he basically said to them, "You just don't get it." Now it seems, considering Peter's response, they just don't get it again. And the time is growing short for them to get it.

Jesus' understanding of his role and ministry symbolized in this act of servitude also shocked the religious leaders who found his understanding and action very disconcerting. He did not fit into their expectations of how God would reveal himself. In fact, it was so disconcerting to their status and role that they helped to engineer his crucifixion. He did not fit the job description that most people, especially the religious leaders, used to look for the Messiah. And it's not really what we expect from the one who is the son of God — a lowly task of washing the disciples' dirty feet.

A messiah wielding a towel and basin is not what we expect.

It was a symbolic moment. It pointed to the nature of Jesus' ministry that was one of being a suffering servant. Jesus set an example for his disciples when he kneeled at their feet and then washed their feet. The posture of his ministry was, and therefore their ministry was, to be one of service, not of status-seeking or power plays or privilege. Likewise, as Christ's followers, the posture for our ministry is kneeling.

In calling people to his ministry, Jesus realized that he needed first to confront the disease endemic to humans — self-centeredness, self-serving, self-deification, selfishness — sin. Self written with a capital S. Before a servant attitude and posture become a real possibility there needs to be a deliverance from the power of sin. To say it in another way, there needs to be a cleansing. Before there can be growth in the spiritual life, there needs to be that point of a new beginning, a new birth, or a birth from above, as the Gospel of John puts it.

But a new birth without growth becomes a stillbirth. John Wesley pointed out that when one accepts Jesus Christ as Savior the process has only just begun. For God in Jesus Christ desires that person to move toward perfection in love and the service of others. It's important to begin with a cleansing. It's an important beginning, an absolutely necessary beginning, but only a beginning.

And such is the message for the church down through the ages. We were created by God to serve. If your life isn't working out for you, it may be that you are not there for others as Christ has called us to be. We are saved from sin and we are saved to serve. E. Stanley Jones called *service to all* one of the six values with which the church is entrusted. Is it one of your values? Do any of us realize anymore that the purpose of life is to praise and serve God and to serve others?

It was a sacred moment. It was a time when the divine dimension openhandedly manifested itself in the human dimension. In the transfiguration there was a sense of the transcendent through the dazzling appearance of Jesus and the presence of Moses and Elijah on the mountaintop with Jesus. That moment on the mountaintop in the transfiguration reeked of the divine. But here the divine was revealed in another, more subtle way through the lowly act of service, and Jesus wants us to know that that moment was just as divine. God comes to his people both in the mountaintop experiences of life, but also even more in the valley experiences where most if us live everyday.

When Jesus took a towel and basin and washed the disciples' feet, he wasn't trying so much to get his disciples or later followers to duplicate his act. What he was after was the kind of person who would have the attitude and posture of a foot washer. What he was after was the kind of person who would be willing to wash another person's feet if that is what is called for. A friend of ours has made it her special mission in life to befriend and visit persons in a nursing home. One day when she was going to transport one of her nursing home friends to a dentist's appointment, this nursing home resident lamented that she always liked to take a bath when she went to such appointments. But a bath was not possible because she was scheduled for two baths a week and this was not her day. She suggested to her friend that if perhaps if she could have her feet washed it would be helpful. And so our friend took a wash cloth, towel, and basin and washed this person's feet because that was what was necessary to be a caring and serving person in this instance. Our friend reported that she welled up with tears because she was overwhelmed by the meaning of the moment. In that moment, the ultimate became intimate, God touched their lives together. For her this scripture passage came to life.

Jesus took a towel and basin and began to wash the disciples' feet. In the dramatic portrayal, Judas realized that in this moment if he had given in, he could have been saved from the terrible morass into which he allowed himself to slide. In this act the heart of God is revealed. "Before we got down to anything important," Judas said. What could have been more important than this singular act in which Jesus communicated to his disciples the cleansing power of his life and death and the servant nature of his ministry?

The Crown Of Thorns

We have been looking at the symbols of the cross during this season. Like the symbols of the rest of the Christian message, these symbols are cumulative. When we put them all together, we see something of the full message of Jesus. The first symbol is the palms which represent the fickleness of the crowd whose Palm Sunday commitment became dry and dead like the palm branches on our cross by the end of the week. The money bag symbolizes on one level greed and on another level the attempt to manipulate Jesus into a different role as Messiah than the one which Jesus understood his role to be. The third symbol, the towel, represents the idea of service. Today we take up another symbol, the crown of thorns and the mockery of Jesus.

In addition to the physical pain and suffering of the cross and the events leading up to the cross that Jesus faced, he also had to endure the rejection, hatred, and mockery of others: Peter denied him. Judas betrayed him. Some disciples fled and others kept their distance. The religious leaders through Caiphas expressed their venom toward Jesus by orchestrating his arrest, trial, and conviction. The political establishment through Pilate played head games with him. And the soldiers mocked him. They formed a crown out of thorns, placed that purple robe around him, and gave him a reed as a scepter. Then they said, "Hail, Jesus, King of the Jews."

What is involved in the act of mockery?

Mockery is a way of dealing with boredom on one level. Mockery can lead to great mischief. Much inhumanity and injustice has been perpetuated throughout history because of boredom. I can imagine that the Roman soldiers found themselves with a great deal of time on their hands waiting around for things to happen. A Roman soldier assigned to the land of Palestine was on the edge of the empire and had a lot of time on his hands. The soldiers played games while they waited for something to happen. In this case the

Roman soldiers filled their boredom with mockery of Jesus. It was just one more game they were playing.

Mockery is one way of keeping the truth at arm's length. We mock what we don't understand. And mockery keeps us from understanding what we ought to understand. And if we don't understand, we don't have to deal with that which we mock. We protect ourselves. We can stay away from life-changing truth. The Roman soldiers certainly did not want to deal with some of the deeper issues of life with which they were confronted by the very presence of Jesus and the claims about him.

Mockery is a way of showing off one's supposed superior status. We are trying to place ourselves in a superior relationship to those whom we mock. Often we do this when in the secret recesses of our lives we actually feel worthless or inferior. Bullies taunt others because at their very heart, they don't feel that good about themselves. They put others down to raise themselves. The Roman soldiers who were assigned to the Palestine contingent were at the bottom of the pecking order. They made themselves feel higher on the ladder by putting down this man Jesus who stood before them. How could he be any kind of king? They'd show the rest. Hail, Jesus, King of the Jews.

Putting a crown of thorns on Jesus was an act of mockery on the part of the soldiers. They acted as if they could make Jesus king as long as they wanted him to be king, and then just as easily take his kingship away. Notice that the soldiers put the crown of thorns and the purple cloak on Jesus and they put the scepter in Jesus' hand. Then they took them all away, as if they had the power to enthrone and dethrone Jesus.

But the interesting thing is that they were right about Jesus in spite of themselves. He was a king, but not the kind of king they were thinking of. He was a king, but not the kind of king they could make or break as they desired. Jesus' kingdom is a kingdom that encompasses this world but also transcends it and a kingdom that operates by a far different set of rules.

We make a mockery of Jesus' kingship in our own lives when we assert Jesus' kingship with our lips but deny his kingship with our lives.

We have a hard time imagining that we could join the soldiers in mocking Jesus. We say to ourselves, we wouldn't have done that. We wouldn't mock Jesus by putting a purple robe on him and a crown of thorns on his head and cynically calling him king. But don't we do something very similar by asserting Jesus' kingship with words but denying him with how we live?

That's what makes walking through this season of Lent with Jesus to the cross so difficult. We think we're rather good people, we're nice people, we don't harm anyone, and we try to do all the good we can, but the goodness of Jesus stands before us and mirrors our lives in such a way that we see how short we have fallen. But the message is not to end on a cynical note. The message all along the way is that we see ourselves in these symbols. We see how we are fickle, and how we too are greedy and would like Jesus to play a different role than the one he has come into our lives with. We see how we would like to avoid the servant role and how much in one way or another we mock Jesus in our own lives by the disparity between what we claim and how we live. The message is that once we see this and admit where we are and who we are, then God's grace can begin to operate in our lives. It's serendipitous once in a while that God's grace and love do break into our lives and we do things that naturally we would not do and we hold back from doing the things we should not do. May God's grace come to us fully through the symbols of the cross so we are empowered for the ministry to which he calls us. Amen.

The Nails

During these Sundays in Lent, we have been looking at the symbols of the cross. It is my hope that these symbols become etched in your minds and hearts to such a degree that you understand the last week in Jesus' life in a new way. You can walk with him to the cross and there see his death and understand his suffering but also participate in his victory over the cross. Look at the cross and its symbols. The fresh palms symbolized the shouting of the crowd, "Hosanna, Hosanna!" as Jesus entered Jerusalem. At the end of the week as the palms died and the people's commitment waned, they shouted, "Crucify him, crucify him." The money bag symbolizes not only the greed that we experience in life but also our attempt to make over Jesus into our image of what we would have him be and do as Messiah. The towel symbolizes Jesus' act of service in washing the disciples' feet and being willing to kneel before others in an act of love to do what they need in that hour. The crown of thorns symbolizes the mocking that Jesus endured. Today we look at the nails of the cross and the suffering of Jesus.

That last week in Jesus' life was quite a week. It began with shouts of "Hosanna!" and ended with cries of "Crucify him!" It began with a triumphal entry and ended on a cross.

✝ Jesus had told his disciples that he must suffer and die, but they just did not understand. He said he must go up to Jerusalem and be delivered up by the chief priest, scribes, and Pharisees and be crucified. So he set his face toward Jerusalem and faced much suffering along the way.

The suffering Jesus experienced was more than a physical suffering. His suffering also involved misunderstanding, betrayal, denial, mockery, abandonment, rejection, and even the sense of being forsaken by God.

We need to recognize there was also a great deal of physical pain and suffering involved: the scourging by the soldiers, the exhaustion of sleepless hours, the wearing trip through the streets to the place of crucifixion, the pounding pain of the nails, the excruciating agony of raising himself to speak on the cross. Jesus indeed faced suffering in all of its dimensions.

A vivid and heart-wrenching description of Jesus' crucifixion and suffering on the cross is in a devotional booklet titled *Reliving The Passion* by Walter Wangerin, Jr.

He writes in the first person:

> *I stand apart. I draw no one's attention. I have covered my head. These are the things I see.*
>
> *I see four soldiers upon a low hill, their greater labor done, their duty now to wait. They are hunching over the few benefits of the morning's assignment. That is, by a grim tradition they can keep the final possessions of those they crucify; so now they're casting lots for an undergarment, a robe, a belt, sandals. No money here. Not even scrip. No matter: the soldiers are passing time. It's nearly noon.*
>
> *A centurion stands over them with his arms folded, gazing up at a coming thunderhead of cloud, squinting, figuring.*
>
> *Above the soldiers, above the centurion, but yet beneath the sun and the lowering cloud, hang three men on crosses each of them stripped to a loin cloth: a robber, a robber, and you.*
>
> *The wind is picking up. Dust blows by. And this is what I see.*
>
> *A wooden board is nailed roughly over your head, chalk white and burned with the indictment: "The King of the Jews." I say, Yes! In my soul I cry, Yes! Yes! I keep my face impassive for fear of the centurion and the chief priests, but Yes, I say, it is what we called the Messiah: King of the Jews! The loutish Romans are right. They mean to mock us, to mock all the Jews as a single people, but their scorn tells the truth, and I take*

a bitter satisfaction in it. Let the chief priests burst their bellies with indignation — I'll just laugh! I hate this world.

But if you're the Messiah, why are you crucified? How can this be? Jesus, Jesus, Jesus, forgive me. My mind rejects the things I see. Nothing fits! I call you King. I call you Master and Lord. You are the Lord! No one has loved as you do — no, not ever, Lord. But I never imagined Goodness to be so broken. Jesus, you grieve me! Jesus, you confuse me —

This is what I see.

Your knees keep buckling. You push yourself up with your legs — to breathe, I think — but the legs lose strength and pop at the knees and your body drops, hah! The arms stretch. The hands clutch spikes. Your shoulder joints separate. Your muscles draw out like ropes. Your rib cage splays. I can count the bones! How do you breathe when your chest is stretched flat? Jesus, you're not breathing! Your own body, when it drags on your arms like that — why your own weight is suffocating you!

Breathe!

Sweet Jesus, please! Breathe!

Make fists on the spike-heads! Lift yourself up. Open your mouth, Lord Jesus, please! Don't die. Don't stop breathing. Breathe! Breathe! ...[1]

Thus Jesus suffered and died on the cross. Why? Why, Lord? Suffering brought Jesus closer to our humanity.

To be human is to experience suffering ...

- There is the suffering caused by our own choices and actions. We bring much suffering on ourselves by our stupid and sinful choices.
- There is the suffering caused by the choices and actions of others. Sometimes we cross paths with those who have made bad choices which affect our lives.
- There is the suffering that comes from living in a world that is made like ours.

29

- Gravity rules in all situations. And if we fall and hurt ourselves, it is the same gravity that keeps us from flying out into space. Jesus experienced the very depth of human suffering. When we pray, we pray to one who knows what it is to suffer.

Suffering brought Jesus closer to God.

- Suffering can either separate a person from God or bring a person closer to God; it can make a person bitter or better.
- In suffering, Jesus was obedient to God's will even though he would have rather taken a different path. *"If it is possible Father, let this cup pass from me but nevertheless not my will but thine be done."*
- In suffering, Jesus threw himself completely into the arms of the God who had seemingly abandon him.
- In suffering, Jesus cried out to God in faith.

Jesus threw himself into the arms of his father, his abba and cried out, *"Father, into thy hands I commend my spirit."*

His suffering and death reveal the depth of our sin and the depth of God's love for us. His suffering and death are the source of our salvation. His suffering and death bring us to God. After we have thrown our very worst at him; he still forgives, he still loves. Oh, the wonder of it all.

> *Upon that cross of Jesus mine eye at times can see*
> *the very dying form of One who suffered there for me;*
> *and from my stricken heart with tears two wonders I*
> *   confess:*
> *the wonders of redeeming love and my unworthiness.*

---

1. Walter Wangerin, Jr., *Reliving The Passion* (Grand Rapids, Michigan: Zondervan Press, 1992)

Five
Who Knew
Jesus

These monologues are dedicated to my wife Carol, whose acceptance of herself as a child of God encourages me to accept my own humanity, and whose compassion inspires me to love and serve.

Introduction

The monologues that follow were originally performed at St. Paul Lutheran Church in Baltimore, Maryland, at midweek services during the Lenten season, 1995. They are designed to enhance the season by reflecting on the personal relationship between Jesus and five who knew him well: John, Mary (the mother of our Lord), Peter, Judas, and Mary Magdalene. By reflecting on each of these personal relationships, individual worshipers are encouraged to look more closely at their own relationship with Christ during the introspective time of Lent.

Each monologue may be done as a readers' theater or, preferably, by memorization. Few, if any, props are needed. Costumes enhance the effect but are not essential. It is suggested that each monologue follow the reading of the scripture and that the pastor briefly introduce each person, focusing on the critical aspect of that person's relationship with Christ. The order is discretionary but we found the following to work very well:

Week 1: John, the hot-tempered young man who became the disciple of love.

Week 2: Mary, Mother of our Lord, who suffers a mother's pain while humbly accepting God's will.

Week 3: Peter, an arrogant man who becomes a humble disciple.

Week 4: Judas, who failed because he thought he knew best.

Week 5: Mary Magdalene, a woman of the world who strove to love herself as Jesus loved her.

Prologue

As we travel with Christ on his forty-day journey to the cross, we again come face to face with the man Jesus. Reflecting on his bitter suffering and death, I am repeatedly overwhelmed by the knowledge that Jesus is not only my risen Savior but that he also walked the earth that I walk, that he faced the temptations that I face, and that he was subject to the pain and suffering common to us all. There was a time in my life when to think of Jesus as a man who became hungry, angry, lonely, tired, doubtful, and frustrated — in words, a man like me — was closely akin to blasphemy. This in spite of my belief in scriptures which clearly say that God became man and dwelt among us. I thank God that in his mercy he chose to reveal his majesty and glory to us in the person of his son. It is only through the incarnate Christ that we, limited as we are by our mortal mind and body, can glimpse the most holy, the unfathomable, I Am. And ironically, it is only through personally relating to the man Christ Jesus that I can fully and lovingly embrace my own humanity.

I find that focusing on Christ's humanity brings me closer and closer to God. It is only through the man Christ Jesus that I can approach God and avail myself of his power and glory. Through Christ, spiritual theory becomes reality. This perspective is especially personal and comforting to me during the Lenten Season. I joyfully anticipate the day when I will see Jesus face to face, when I shall know him fully even as I am fully known. But for the time being, I see through a glass darkly and eagerly welcome any light that will illuminate my darkness. Jesus promised that if we seek, we shall find. It is an undisputable truth that the grace of God can bring us understanding and insight; it is equally undisputable to me that if we seek to know the man Jesus, we will come to walk more closely with him and we will come to know personally, by the evidence of our senses, many of the joys and blessings we once merely accepted on faith. Jesus will become a true and present friend, not someone confined to the pages of books or sequestered within places of worship.

As I sought to deepen my own relationship with Christ, I began prayerfully to consider some of the important relationships individuals had with our Savior during his earthly sojourn. *Five Who Knew Jesus* considers relationships with Christ from the personal points of view of individuals who played important roles in the life of Christ: John, the hot-tempered young man who became the disciple of love; Mary, the Mother of our Lord, who suffered a mother's pain while humbly accepting God's will; Peter, an arrogant man who became a humble disciple; Judas, who failed because he thought he knew best; and Mary Magdalene, a woman of the world who strove to love herself as Jesus did. Each played a critical role in the life of Christ; each brought his/her own individual strengths, weaknesses, hopes, and fears to the relationship, just as we, as followers of Christ, bring our selves to our relationship with him. As we consider each testimony, perhaps we can see ourselves in each of the five, for better or for worse. And perhaps we will become more willing to have our rough edges tempered, our ego deflated, our own will subjugated, and our passion redirected. Perhaps, unlike Judas, we will realize that we do not know best and, rather than relying on our own knowledge and understanding, we will always come to look to Jesus, the author and finisher of our faith. To God be the glory.

Harold D. Shaffer

John

The Sea of Galilee is so beautiful; I wish I were there now, with Jesus and Peter and James and the others. Those were some of the happiest days of my life. Instead, I am here. Here on this hill above Jerusalem — hiding. I often come here to pray and think of how my life has changed. For years the only place where I felt at peace was on the Sea of Galilee. And it's no coincidence that it was there at that lakeside where my life really began when I began following Jesus. But tonight I could have no peace anywhere this side of heaven. I fear what awaits my Master who, even now, stands before Pilate as a prisoner of the Romans while I, his beloved disciple, stand a free man on this hillside to which I fled.

My mother, Salome, is a sister of Mary, the mother of Jesus. I didn't hang around with Jesus while we were growing up. I was busy on the fishing boats while he was learning to be a carpenter from my uncle Joseph. James and I were very different from Jesus. While he was learning a quiet trade and studying the Law of the Prophets, James and I were hanging out with the rough men of the sea and getting into trouble at every turn. I see now that I was a perfect example of self-will run riot. No one could tell me anything and pity the person who stood in my way. I can still hear my mother pleading for James and me to be more like our cousin.

I am a fisherman and have spent my life near the water. As with life, the Sea of Galilee is not always calm and beautiful. At times the west wind funnels down through the gap across the flat plain of Gennesaret and whips up the surface of the sea. The wind can come quickly anytime, even at midday. More than once I've stood on the deck of our fishing boat and cursed the ten-foot waves which threatened to swamp us. When storms came upon us, and the thunder crashed and the lightning filled the sky, we would seek a safe harbor. One night, we were traveling with Jesus on the Sea of Galilee, when a great storm came on the sea. Our ship was covered with waves and we were sure that we would perish. We woke Jesus, who was sleeping peacefully in the back of the ship, and pleaded with him to save us. He looked at us and said: "Why are you fearful, you of little faith?" He raised his arms to the sea and said, "Peace, be still," and there came a great calm. I often think of that time. I boomed like thunder and struck like lightning, and created a life that left me a floundering vessel, beaten and battered. Christ quieted the storm that was my life and became my great harbor of refuge. He looked at me and said, "Peace, be still."

But wait, I am getting ahead of myself. It was about three years ago that a cousin of Jesus suddenly came out of the wilderness, proclaiming the coming of the Messiah and preaching baptism of repentance for the forgiveness of sins. This man's name was also John. Zealots were not new to us but John was somehow different; I heard him preach several times. When he spoke of the Kingdom of God, his eyes burned like fiery coals and his voice boomed like thunder; and when he spoke of the Messiah, I felt a peace I had never known. I was at the Jordan when John baptized Jesus and hailed him as the Messiah. That's when I first thought that maybe Jesus was the promised one. Not wanting to be thought a fool, I kept my thoughts to myself and went about my business.

One morning, a short time after Jesus was baptized, James and I, along with our father and crew were in our boats mending nets. Jesus came by with Andrew and Peter. I was wondering what they were doing together when Jesus looked into my eyes and said, "Come with me." All doubts disappeared. It was clear that I was meant to follow this man. James told me later that it was as though God, himself, had spoken. We left our father in the boat and followed Jesus. The four of us went with him to the synagogue at Capernaum. From there we went to Simon Peter's house, which became our headquarters in Galilee. As Jesus came to know James and me, he nicknamed us "Boanerges" which means "sons of thunder." As I said before, I had a violent temper. Once when we were in Capernaum, I stopped a man from casting out devils in the name of Jesus. I proudly told Jesus what I had done. Instead of praising me, Jesus rebuked me, saying that whoever works a miracle in

39

Jesus' name would not speak evil of him. Now, when I look back I am ashamed of my arrogance and hot temper. I am even more ashamed of the time that James and I asked Jesus to reserve the seats on his left and right for us in his Kingdom. It is said, and will later be recorded by some, that it was our mother who requested that Christ honor James and me with exalted positions. It was not our mother who sought recognition for us. James and I, moved by our pride of achievement and satisfaction with our accomplishments, made the request. Those who say otherwise are trying to protect our reputation. My face burns when I recall Jesus telling us that those positions were not his to give. God have mercy on me, a miserable sinner.

Walking with Jesus, I experienced his word as truth and I received the blessings and the joy of his love. His pardon was full and free. By his example and encouragement, I found myself wanting to be more like him. Although I did not feel worthy, Jesus took me, along with James and Peter, into his inner circle. We three alone were blessed to accompany him when he healed Jairus' daughter; we witnessed the glory of his transfiguration on the mountain; and he took us with him to the Garden of Gethsemane. I came to know by the evidence of my senses what I first took on faith.

Earlier tonight in the Upper Room, we celebrated Passover. Jesus washed our feet. He then looked at us and said that one of us would betray him, and he let it be known who this would be. He told us that he would only be with us for a little while and that we could not go where he was going. He then rose and said: "A new commandment I give to you, that you love one another as I have loved you, and by this shall all men know that you are my disciples." We had the commandments which God had given to Moses on the mountain those many years ago. But now we had a new commandment, one given to us personally by God's own son; given to us by the Divine Image of love which sat before us in the person of the man, Christ Jesus.

Jesus' words were alive in my heart as we set out for the Garden of Gethsemane after supper. I pledged to myself to love as he loved, remembering his promise that all who keep his commandments shall abide in his love. And now, on this night, he had given us a new commandment. I felt refreshed in body and renewed in spirit. And yet — and yet, it was as Jesus said: The spirit is willing but the flesh is weak. I prayed for God's blessings and for strength but where was I tonight when Jesus came to bless me? I slept when he asked me to watch; I cowered in fear when the soldiers took him. I felt strongly one way and acted another. I prefer to measure myself by my intentions, but I must judge myself and be judged by my actions.

I forgot the Master's promises. My resolve ripped open and my faith scattered like so many straws in the wind. Oh, my soul, be still. Without Christ I can do nothing; with him I am empowered to do all things. And now, standing here on this hillside, praying and pondering my Master's love, the peace of God is returning. "Love one another as I love you": the great commandment. Abiding in Christ's love, I have strength for every duty, courage for every struggle. I fear what awaits my Master, but I know in whom I believe. He is the one who transformed the Son of Thunder into the Beloved. From the moment he invited me to go with him, he opened his arms and took me to his bosom; he opened his heart and welcomed me there; and he opened up the fullness of life and love and made me one with him. Abiding in his love, I have a blessing in every cross and the joy of life eternal in death. I will be with him today and through my love, made possible by God's grace, all men shall know that I am his disciple.

TO GOD BE THE GLORY

Mark 3:31-35
 # 494

Mary
(The Mother Of Our Lord)

Little did I know growing up in Nazareth of Galilee that I had been chosen by God to be his sacred vessel. Although my family devoutly kept the Law of Moses, there was nothing to foretell the great blessing that would be bestowed upon us. Neither my father, Joachim, nor my mother, Anne, were of the families of any of Israel's great prophets or leaders. From the time I was a young girl, I loved to wander through the hills and around our village. When I was fourteen, my father arranged for me to marry Joseph, a well-respected carpenter of the House of David. After my engagement, I took more notice of the children of the village when I was on my walks. I began thinking of what it would be like to be a mother. As I watched the children laugh and play, I imagined what kind of people they would grow up to be. Would my daughters marry well and have many children? Would my sons be fishermen or craftsmen? Perhaps they would be great teachers or even prophets. And, of course, the dream of all dreams: Like most of my friends, I hoped to be the one chosen by God to give birth to the Messiah. Just the thought of being the one was almost too much to bear.

One evening as I lay in bed thinking of my approaching marriage, a light suddenly appeared in my room. It became brighter and brighter until it overtook the darkness and left me lying in brilliant light. As I watched trembling, a form appeared at the foot of my bed, looked at me, and said: "Hail, full of grace, the Lord is with thee. Blessed art thou among women." I sat up in my bed, pulled the blanket tightly to my chin, and asked this stranger what he meant. He told me not to be afraid, that I had been chosen by God to give birth to a son, and that I should call him Jesus. I asked how this could be, since I was a virgin. The stranger said that the Holy Ghost would come upon me. Although I was confused and

42

afraid, I knew that this person of light was an angel from God. "I am the Lord's servant," I said. "God's will be done."

During his visit, the angel told me that my relative Elizabeth would also have a child. This was a great surprise since everyone thought that she was barren. I hurried to Elizabeth's home. When she saw me coming, she ran down the path, hugged me, and said that the child I carried and I were blessed. As we walked to her house, Elizabeth asked why I, the mother of our Lord, had come to visit. I told her what the angel had said. As I spoke, Elizabeth began weeping with joy and told me that when she had heard my voice, her child had leaped in her womb. We knew that we had been blessed by God and believed that our children were chosen for a specific mission. We wondered what awaited them. We were also afraid. Many called by God suffer greatly because the ways of God are not the ways of man.

Upon my return to Nazareth, I learned that Joseph, too, had had a heavenly visitor and knew that the child I carried was the Son of God. Shortly afterward, Joseph and I went to Bethlehem to be counted in the census. By this time, I was heavy with child. As we arrived in Bethlehem, my time had come. Joseph searched desperately for a place to stay but there was no room. Finally a kindly innkeeper, hearing of my condition, offered us a stall in his stable. There, among the cows and sheep, my son Jesus was born. When a few days old, we took him to the temple in Jerusalem to be dedicated. In the temple there was a man called Simeon. When Simeon saw us, he took Jesus in his arms and praised God. He blessed us and said that Jesus was the Promised One. Simeon then took me aside and told me that although I was blessed, a sword would pierce my soul. Simeon's words filled my heart with a fear that I have carried to this very day. As we left the temple, an old prophetess in the temple began praising God and saying that Jesus was the Redeemer. Since the angel's visit I have been blessed, but also burdened, by the knowledge that Jesus was sent by God. I pray that God will continue to grant me the grace to accept his will and to bear the burden in silent love.

Like any other child, Jesus grew up at my side. I taught him to speak and to say his first prayers. I told him stories and made sure

43

he took his naps, singing to him softly until his eyelids drooped and I could lay him in his bed. As he grew, he followed me around the house, asking never-ending questions. Although loving and respectful, there was always distance between Jesus and me. He was wise beyond his years and my relationship to him was not typical of a mother to her son. How could it be? He spoke of God as his true father. I marveled at my son's insight and wondered at his mission and purpose. And always I was haunted by Simeon's words.

When Jesus was twelve, we took our yearly journey to Jerusalem for Passover. As we were returning home, we discovered that Jesus was not with us. We were frantic and hurried back to Jerusalem, fearing the worst. After three days, we found him in the temple, sitting with the teachers and amazing them with his knowledge and understanding. I was relieved, but angry, and I rushed to him crying and told him that we had been searching everywhere for him. Jesus looked at me and asked why we were looking for him. Didn't we know that he had to be about his father's business? His words stung me like the hot desert sand. Joseph led me away, bewildered and heartbroken. It was as though a sword had pierced my heart. Shortly afterward, Jesus joined us and stayed with us until he began preaching. I worried about him as he began what now seems to be the last leg of his journey, a journey I know he must travel alone. Oh, but if I could only walk with my son every step of the way. But it is not to be. I pray for knowledge of God's will for me and the power to carry it out.

I know my son is the Promised One and I have been blessed to share his life. I have kept all that I have seen and heard in my heart, and know that the time will come when I must let him go. That knowledge and Jesus' understanding of his mission kept us separate even while we were together. At the marriage feast at Cana, while I did play a part, Jesus, as he did in the temple those many years ago, made clear his mission and calling. When he addressed me as "woman" I was hurt, not only by his words but by his tone. It was a sword through my heart. Yes, he is my son. But more importantly, he is my Savior. I have told myself that many times to help me deal with what I feel as rejection. I know he loves me. It's just that sometimes I want him to be just my son, and not the Messiah. Perhaps I am selfish. But he is my son and I love him.

I haven't seen much of Jesus during the past three years as he went about preaching and performing miracles, but I have thought of him constantly and feared for his safety. The Romans are suspicious of anyone with a following and have killed more than one man for inciting rebellion. Now I know that the chief priests and teachers of the synagogue are an even greater threat to Jesus. They have accused him of blasphemy and threatened his life. Tonight I learned that Jesus was taken in chains from the Garden to the high priest and has been condemned to die. Even now I hear the mob. I must join him. I cannot let my son die alone. As a believer, I pray that God's will be done; as a mother, I weep for my son.

TO GOD BE THE GLORY

Five Who Knew Jesus

Matt 26:69-75
Father, I adore You "

Peter

I denied him! I denied him! I denied him. It would be better had I never been born, or that I had stayed under the water where I sank when I took my eyes off of Jesus that night on the Sea of Galilee. I, the Big Fisherman, who no man dares cross and to whom Jesus looked to lead the others. I, whose rough manners and boastful ways were tempered by the gentle and humble bearing of the Christ. I, the coward, lives, and he, the strongest and bravest of all men, shall die a brutal death. Yes, Jesus will die today. I could have stopped it from happening. Rock? Rock? I am no more than a pebble; I am less than the dust to which I shall return, none too soon. Better that I had died as Simon, the son of John, than to have failed Jesus as Peter, the Rock. And what of the rest of the twelve who were called? Only John, the Beloved, stayed with the Master.

It is as though it were only yesterday that, as my brother Andrew and I were netting fish in Lake Galilee, Jesus walked by. Of course I knew who he was because Andrew had told me that John the Baptist had greeted Jesus as the Lamb of God. Andrew had come to me so excited that he could barely talk. "Simon! Simon!" he had cried. "We have found the Messiah." Well, I'll tell you, I had my doubts. Sure, I knew that the Prophets said that one day a Messiah would come. And in spite of what some people would say about my vulgar manner, I was a devout keeper of the Law of Moses. I had hoped that I would live to see the Christ, but as I watched my life speed by I had begun to wonder. But that day by the lake, when Jesus looked at Andrew and me and said, "Come with me and I will teach you to catch men," we at once left our nets and went with him to become fishers of men. Little did I know what awaited me. When Jesus said, "Follow me!" I followed. For a while after that, I wondered why I obeyed him. It was not in my nature to permit any man to tell me what to do. I came to see that it was the grace of God that led me to leave my nets and the occupation that I loved.

Not long after we began following Jesus, while we were still in our own village accompanying Jesus as he preached in the synagogues, my wife's mother took seriously ill with a deadly sickness. We tried everything, but it looked as though she would surely die. We told Jesus of her condition, and he went home with us. He sat by my mother-in-law's bed, took her hand, and bowed his head. He then helped her sit up, and she opened her eyes and smiled. She immediately left her bed and prepared supper for us. It was truly a miracle. Because of his preaching and his miracles, the hypocrites in power sought ways to catch him in the net of blasphemy. The miracles Jesus performed convinced me that he was surely sent from God: I was there when he cured the man of leprosy, and the centurion's servant with palsy, and the woman who suffered twelve years with an issue of blood, and the daughter of Jarius, and the man with the withered hand, and so many others. Having seen, it was not so difficult to believe.

I want to believe that I would have accepted Jesus as the Christ even if I had not seen him perform a single miracle. But I must remain ever mindful of my inflated opinion of myself and of my capacities. I like to think that I am not like other men: that my faith is greater, that my mind is sharper, and that I am not subject to the many temptations with which others, including the Christ, are assailed by the devil. Ah, sometimes we learn slowly of the subtlety and power of our foe. As I was saying, apart from the miracles he performed, Jesus' words alone set him far above any prophet who ever lived. He spoke in stories that were foolishness to those who did not believe, but to us who believed his words were salvation unto God.

Soon after our calling, Jesus took the twelve of us to the hills around Caesarea Philippi. There he taught us for many days, away from the rantings of the Pharisees and the distractions of the crowds that had come to follow him everywhere. One morning as we sat reflecting, each of us on his own thoughts, Jesus looked at us and asked who the people thought he was. Andrew replied that some said he was John the Baptist, and Thomas said that others believed he was Elijah or Jeremiah or one of the other prophets. Then Jesus said, "Who do you say I am?" We all looked at one another, each afraid to speak. Of course I, self-proclaimed leader that I was, spoke up. "You are the Christ!" I thundered, proud that I, alone among the twelve, had the insight and the courage to take a stand. Among the frightful mumbling of the eleven, Jesus looked directly at me. He seemed both shocked and pleased. "Peter," he said, "flesh and blood did not reveal this to you, but my Father who is in heaven." Maybe so, I thought, but I had something to do with it.

After acknowledging that he is the Son of God, Jesus told all of us to tell no man what we heard. He also told us that he must go to Jerusalem. There he would be persecuted and killed, but would be raised again on the third day. I, Peter, the Rock, could not permit this.

"God forbid, Lord!" I shouted. "I will not let this happen to you." Jesus grabbed me by the shoulders and shook me. It was one of the few times I ever saw him angry. He shouted at me, "Get behind me, Satan! You are a hindrance and an offense to me, for your thoughts are not of God, but of man!" Looking back, I realize that it was at that moment that I experienced firsthand the devil as the adversary of the children of God. I came to see that of myself I am powerless over the forces of darkness. I can resist Satan and his angels only by remaining steadfast in the faith.

Although I now have a better understanding of what happened, I admit that I was frightened when Jesus rebuked the devil within me. I meant no harm. I wanted him to know that I loved him and would protect him. Jesus, as only he could do, sensed my fear and pain, put his arms around me, looked into my eyes, and spoke to us all: "If any man will come after me, let him deny himself and take up his cross, and follow me. For whosoever will save his life shall lose it; and whosoever will lose his life for my sake shall find it. For what does it profit a man if he gains the whole world and loses his own soul?"

Indeed. Oh, what bitter irony? I have saved myself and lost my soul. To think that I, one of the Master's inner circle; I, the first to acknowledge him as Messiah; I, upon whose profession Christ built his church; I, Peter, the Rock, denied Jesus not once but three times.

And after I denied him the third time, I heard the cock crow. At that moment, I was of all men the most miserable. How can he forgive me? I denied him today out of fear, but what about last night? Although he asked us to keep watch, I couldn't even stay awake when he went to pray in the Garden. And before that, when he spoke to us after supper, he told us that very night we would all fall away from him and that he would be taken. When Jesus said that, I hugged him to me and boasted that while the others might run, I would never leave him. That's when he leaned close to me; I could feel his breath and his tears. He whispered in my ear, "Verily, I say unto you, that this night, before the cock crows you will deny me three times." "Never!" I said. "I will die before I deny you." Jesus just smiled sadly.

Later that night the mob came to Gethsemane to take Jesus. I, overcome by guilt at having slept on my watch, seized a sword and cut off an ear of a servant of the high priest. I announced that I was ready to die for my Master, but upon reflection I question my motive. How much of my action was out of love and loyalty and how much out of a need to bandage my ego, wounded by the humiliation at having fallen asleep? Perhaps my bravery would lead Jesus to overlook my failing him. Even at that most tragic of times I was thinking of myself first. Jesus' only response was to tell me to put my sword away. He then said that all who draw the sword will die by the sword. He looked at me and seemed surprised that I didn't understand what was happening. "Don't you know that I could call upon my father to rescue me?" He asked. He then said what should have been obvious to a follower as devoted as I: "But how then would the scriptures be fulfilled?" Jesus then placed the severed ear back onto the servant's head, and the guards took him away. They also took James, John, and me, but as the three of us were led away, a priest held his lantern close to our faces. When he saw who we were, he spat on us and told the guards to let us go. Caiaphas only wanted Jesus; we three were nobody. As they led Jesus away, I followed at a distance.

Now I stand alone. The sun is rising but the day is dark. I hear the cries of the mob in the city, carried on a dry wind that blows through my tattered cloak and chills my very soul. Surely, as Jesus said, the shepherd is stricken and the sheep are scattered. God have mercy on us all.

TO GOD BE THE GLORY

Judas

Why do you look at me that way in your smug self-righteousness? I, Judas Iscariot, loved him more than any of you ever could love him; it's just that I love Israel more. I don't know why I would expect anything but contempt from you. After all, I've never gotten the respect I deserve. No, I wasn't like the others. I'm not good and pure like the beloved John. Nor would I boast of bravery and leadership while following along like a sheep, like that big-mouth Peter. But I, above all of the others, was loyal to Israel and I know the scriptures. I knew what was best and did what I had to do. I don't expect you to understand. You weren't there. It's easy to sit back and judge a battle when you're not in the trenches. It's easy to talk about love and forgiveness when you don't have to face hate and oppression every day of your life.

I still don't understand why we had to go through this. As far as I was concerned, and I tried to convince Jesus, we could overthrow the Romans with the forces of heaven. Just last Sunday we had the perfect opportunity for Jesus to ascend to power. As we traveled to Jerusalem to observe Passover, thousands of people greeted us. When they saw Jesus coming down the path on a donkey, the sight reminded them of the prophecy of Zechariah: "Shout, O daughter of Jerusalem; Behold, your king comes to you. He is triumphant and victorious, lowly, and riding upon an ass." And the crowd pulled olive branches off the trees and began to hail Jesus as the son of David, and their king. As we approached the temple, the chief priests were furious at seeing the people acclaiming Jesus and demanded that it stop. I knew beyond any doubt that the priests saw Jesus' popularity too threatening and would take steps to put an end to it all. As I said, that was our opportunity. Why wait for the priests to make a move? I actually thought that on that day, in response to the cries of the crowd, Jesus would climb the temple stairs, seize a sword, and proclaim his kingdom. But no. Jesus said that the prophecy must be fulfilled. He said it again, two days before Passover. That's when he told us that he must be handed over to be crucified. I didn't really believe he would let it happen. I just knew that once he was about to be taken he would call down legions of angels to destroy his enemies. That would be what I've been waiting for and it would be the sign for our people to rise up, overthrow our oppressors, and establish God's Kingdom on earth. Isn't that what the Prophets predicted? Didn't they say that a Messiah would come to set up his Kingdom? I've been waiting for a Jewish Kingdom all of my life. I have followed several would-be Messiahs in my lifetime, hoping against hope that each was the One. After each of them was killed or ran away, I saw them for what they were — impostors.

But this Jesus — I truly thought he was the Promised One. When he told us that he must be handed over to his enemies, I thought he was telling us to arrange for his capture so that he could then finally reveal his power and glory. Why do you look at me that way? Is it hate? Or is it pity? Don't you believe what I'm saying? I went to the chief priests because Jesus wanted to be handed over. I had to force the issue. What about the thirty pieces of silver, you ask. I had to make the priests believe that I was serious; that I would betray Jesus for gain. If I had not asked for money, they would have suspected something; they know my reputation as a manager of money. I didn't need a measly thirty pieces of silver. After all, do you forget that I served as treasurer for our group of disciples? That brings me to something else: If I were not trustworthy, would Jesus have selected me to be treasurer?

Oh, sure, my attempts to keep money in our coffers sometimes got me into trouble. Like the time when we were at the home of Simon the Leper in Bethany. That woman, who always seemed to be hanging around, came to Jesus with an alabaster jar of very expensive perfume. At first, I thought that she was making a contribution. But no, she poured it on Jesus' head. I couldn't believe my eyes. I tried to grab the perfume from her. "You fool," I said. "Don't waste this. We can sell the perfume for a high price and give the money to the poor." I thought Jesus would commend me for being so frugal. But he looked at me, that way he often did, and ordered me to leave the woman alone. He said that the poor will always be with us but that he would not. Jesus then told us that the woman poured the perfume on his body to prepare him for burial. That is when I knew what I had to do.

After meeting with the priests, it was just a matter of time before I would give them their opportunity. Jesus knew this. That's why tonight at supper he told me to go and do what I must. But before that, just to show how much he loved me, he had me sit beside him during the meal. He even dipped his bread in the wine and gave me the sop. He would only do that for one he loved. Anyway, I knew he was going to the Garden after the meal. When I left the supper, I went and told the priests, who brought the temple guards to arrest Jesus. I had arranged a signal with them: the one I kissed would be the man. When we arrived in the garden, torches burning and excitement high, I went up to Jesus. "Greetings, Rabbi!" I said. Jesus looked at me and said, "Friend, do what you came for." I kissed him and the guards seized him. That's when I expected Jesus to call upon his father to rescue him and set up his Kingdom on earth. It didn't happen. He let himself be led away and wouldn't allow anyone to resist. Although there wasn't much that John and Peter could do to protect him, to his credit, the bigmouth did grab a sword and cut off an ear of one of the temple guards. But Jesus picked up the ear and placed it back on the guard's head. Will I ever understand?

There's a lot I don't understand; like the Kingdom of Heaven that Jesus was always talking about. I wasn't interested in the Kingdom of Heaven. I wanted the Kingdom of Israel, just as God intended when he gave this land to his chosen people. There would be time enough for a Kingdom of Heaven after we threw out the scum of Rome, those heathens who deny Jehovah and worship pagan gods with the blood of Jews. Why did Jesus not take up the sword and lead us to victory? So many times I pleaded with him to seize his destiny. He would smile at me and say, "My dear Judas, change your heart. Love your enemies and heaven and earth will embrace. We are all brothers. The journey to heaven is a path of love." Jesus was such a dreamer. There is only one true path: the deliverance of Israel!

I did what I had to do. Didn't I? Tell me I did. Please tell me. When Jesus let himself be taken, I still had some hope. But when he was handed over to Pilate and then condemned to death, I knew that it was all over. Oh, my God, what have I done? I was sure that I knew what was best. This was not in my plan. I went to the priests. I told them that I sinned — that I had betrayed innocent blood. I prayed that they would release Jesus. They laughed at me. I threw the money at them and ran away. Now, here I stand, guilty. Guilty! Guilty! If only I could tell Jesus that I'm sorry, that I did what I thought was best. But now it's too late. I know why you look at me that way. I am a pitiful creature. I have killed the most loving person I ever knew and still cannot bring myself to ask for forgiveness. Tomorrow, Jesus will hang in glory from a cross; tonight, I will hang in shame from a tree.

TO GOD BE THE GLORY

John 19:16b-25
347

Mary Magdalene

Unloved and unlovable. The woman I was a few short years ago would not be standing before you tonight sharing the love of Jesus and the saving grace of God. Even if I had wanted to be in this house of worship, you would not have permitted the woman I was to have stood before you. I don't blame you if you still have doubts about me. I sometimes doubt myself and think that my new life in Christ is all a dream, that the miracle of redemption did not occur, and that I will return to my iniquity. But when these thoughts come to me, I think of Jesus and know the miracle of being a new creature in him.

I recognize some of you; you who, when you saw me on the street, would cross to the other side. You, men and women together, who publicly scorned me and wanted to stone me to death for my sins. And, yes, I see some of you men who now turn away, hoping that I will not see you. Those of you who condemned me and yet sought out me pleasures in the dark of night. Be that as it may. I now stand before you, a miracle. I, who judged myself much more harshly than any of you ever could; I, a prisoner of the flesh within me and convinced that I was unworthy to be forgiven, live now as a devoted follower of Jesus.

I am a Galilean from the city of Magdala. You know the place. It is an important trading center at the southern end of the Plain of Gennesaret. Many wealthy merchants pass through our city with money to spend on women and wine. I was available and was sought out because of my reputation. I drank with the best of them and gave myself totally to lust. No depravity was beyond me, for I was slave to the demons that possessed me. I lived only for pleasure and for the joy of possessing the money and gifts given to me by men. But the day came when there was neither joy nor pleasure. I became consumed by guilt and broken in spirit. I had neither the strength nor courage to break away from the life I led. It was at the point of total despair, when I thought often of taking my own life to end my wretched sickness of soul, that I was approached by some women who were followers of a new prophet in Galilee. You can imagine my surprise to find that anyone, especially women, were concerned for my soul. And yet Johanna, the wife of Herod's business manager, and Susanna, a prominent woman of Galilee, and other women of means who had been physically and spiritually supporting the prophet and his disciples, pleaded with me to go with them to hear Jesus. I was reluctant; I knew I was hopeless. But then James, one of the disciples of the prophet, came to see me. I fully expected him to condemn me; condemnation was all that I had ever known. Instead, James treated me kindly and encouraged me to hear Jesus speak, at least once. I was so sick in body and soul that it was only with the love and acceptance of James, and the support of the women that I was able to set out to see this man Jesus. I now know that if I had anywhere else to turn, I would certainly not have turned to a man who many branded a fanatic and worse.

Jesus was speaking on a mountain, just beyond Gabara. Crowds were camped around the hillside and there were scores of the sick and the lame, and those possessed by demons. Because of my shame, I tried to hide in the crowd but my friends pushed me forward so that I could better see and hear. When I first saw Jesus, I was struck by his appearance. It was not so much that he was handsome. I had been with many men much more handsome than he. But when he looked at me, I felt that he could see into my very soul. His eyes were so filled with a love and understanding that I could not turn away, although that was my inclination. It had been a very long time since I had been able to look into the eyes of anyone. Jesus was so mild in manner and yet spoke with such power and authority that he held the attention of the most impatient and unruly. He quoted the Prophets and spoke of repentance. He proved the coming of the Messiah by explaining how the Old Testament prophecies had been fulfilled. He spoke with great love and respect of John the Baptist, who he said had prepared his way. And then Jesus spoke of sin. He listed the vices of the people, our hypocrisy, our apathy, our pride, and our idolatry of the sinful flesh. When he spoke, especially of the sinful flesh, I cringed. I was too aware of my sins and, at that moment, I realized that this man also knew everything that there was to know about my life. It was as though he was speaking directly to me. I then expected to be condemned, but instead, with a love I had never known, Jesus invited all sinners to come to him. He implored God to touch the hearts of people that even one, though burdened by guilt, would come to him. With tears in his eyes, he said he would give all — yes, even his life — to purchase one soul. I wanted to go to him when he reached out to me in my pain and isolation. But I was too ashamed to accept the gift he so freely offered.

Although I couldn't bring myself to go to Jesus, neither could I let him walk out of my life. Several other women and I followed him to the home of Simon the Pharisee who had invited him to dinner. As Jesus sat down to eat, I surprised myself by boldly pushing through the crowd of men. I clutched in my hand a bottle of expensive perfume which I had brought with me and which I intended to give to him as a gift. Despite the grumblings, I let nothing hold me back. I had seen hope in the person and the words of Jesus. When I reached him, I knelt at his feet, crying. My tears were a prayer which Jesus heard. My tears fell on his feet and I wiped them with my hair and kissed them. I was so overcome with joy and wanted somehow to show him my love. I poured the perfume on his feet. When Simon saw Jesus permitting me to honor him in this way, he shouted that this proved that Jesus was not who he claimed to be. For if he were, he would know what kind of a woman I was and would condemn me instead of letting me minister to him. Jesus turned to Simon and said that he had not shown Jesus the courtesy of offering him water to wash the dust from his feet and, yet, that I had washed his feet with my tears and dried them with my hair; that Simon had neglected the courtesy of olive oil to anoint his head but that I had covered his feet with expensive perfume. Jesus then said that my sins — which were many — were forgiven, for I loved him much. He turned to the crowd sitting at dinner and told them that one who is forgiven little, shows little love. Jesus then helped me to my feet, looked deeply into my eyes, and told me that my sins were forgiven. He held my hand and said that my faith had saved me and for me to go in peace.

I didn't know what to make of this man. He loved me unconditionally; me, who had never known love and had despaired of ever being accepted and loved for who I am. I had always been the object of lust and base desires. When Jesus forgave me, I felt forgiven and longed to be with him always. My heart was full of Christ, and my love could be satisfied with nothing short of Jesus. I accompanied him throughout Galilee and, along with several other women, cared for his needs and those of his followers. Jesus and the twelve had no means of support because they had devoted their life to furthering the Kingdom of God. The fishermen had left their nets, the farmers their fields, and Jesus, himself, had put aside his carpenter tools. Were it not for the women of Galilee, these brave and dedicated men would have often gone hungry. I am continually amazed by the reality that the eternal God became a man who walked the earth. I am still trying to accept and understand the truth about Christ and his mission. He has said that he will not be with us very long. Yet, he said that he will be with us always. I am often confused but I know that I don't have to understand to believe. I don't understand how I could became a new person, more in the likeness of Jesus; but that's exactly what happened. I live to be his disciple and to learn to love him as he loves me.

TO GOD BE THE GLORY

Carl B. Rife has pastored United Methodist congregations throughout Maryland and Pennsylvania for more than thirty years. A graduate of United Theological Seminary (M.Div.) and Wesley Theological Seminary (D.Min.), Rife also served for three years on the staff at United Theological Seminary. His sermons and worship resources have appeared in several CSS publications, and he is the author of *Bumper Sticker Religion* (CSS).

An active member of St. Stephen Lutheran Church in Arbutus, Maryland, **Harold D. Shaffer** is a licensed clinical counselor who currently serves on the staff of an addictions clinic in Catonsville, Maryland. Shaffer is also on the adjunct faculty of Baltimore City Community College and the Maryland Office of Education and Training for Addiction Services (OETAS). He is a graduate of Loyola (Md.) College.